Five Kootenay Lake Poets

All rights reserved. No part of this book may be used or reproduced in any manner whatsoever without written permission except in the case of brief quotations in a review. For further information, please contact the publisher, Eva Nova Press.

Copyright ©2016 by the individual poets: Mark Mealing, Anne Heard, Sheila Murray-Nellis, Robert Banks Foster, Sheila Falle

Cover photograph by Mark Mealing.

ISBN: 978-0-9951941-2-0

Eva Nova Press

PO Box 313

Kaslo, BC V0G 1M0

Canada

For our families

Mark Mealing

I. Traditions.

Coyote Up There

So I'm walking along, eh?
& somebody calls, Hey!
 & I look about
but don't see no one

                      Up here!
& I look up this time
& there's Coyote
                way up in the sky
                      among them clouds.
       Coyote! I says
What're you doing up there?
I just come up, says Coyote,
I go everywhere.
Yeah, but Coyote,
        I says
        You never been up there before.
So? says Coyote,
      I'm up here now
        I don't have to go always the same place
          & I don't like ruts
            You run along a rut, you could get stuck in the mud
& when I'm in a hurry from where I been
          if I get stuck in a rut
them back there, they'll catch up with me
                      Hoo! never want that.

   OK, Coyote, I says
but how you get up there?
Well, I just come, says Coyote
      I was looking up & now here I am
Come on up!

    It's pretty nice up here

But everyone can see you up there
I says
    including them angry folks
        back from where you come from
Yeah, yeah says Coyote
    but I can see them too
   In fact, I can see a lot of them that doesn't see me
Come on up!

    & I think it might be pretty nice
& then, all of a sudden I'm up there beside him
    up in the clouds
       big & soft & white
      & full of light

So I try to sit on one
Hey! I says
   it's all wet
  I'm soaked
Where do you think rain comes from
says Coyote
   not from desert sands down there
       like they got in Osoyoos
   these is clouds
of course they're wet

  So what am I going to sit on
I says
& Coyote:
   sit on the air
   like me
you can't sit on air, I says
    it's air

you can't sit on it
      Well, what am I sitting on then
says Coyote
      & it's true

So I sits down
but of course the air don't hold me
 & I end up on my arse
Look at that
      I says, grumbling
you can't sit on air
Well, says Coyote
      what're you sitting on now?

So I looks down
      & it's true
I'm sitting on the air
& I looks down
& there's the mountains & that big lake of ours
                    way down below
                    WAY way down

Hoo! I says
      I'm really high
It has that effect
      says Coyote
         always willing to misunderstand

How we gonna get down?
I says
& Coyote gets all sheepish
I di'n't work that out yet
              he says

& I get mad

You mean we're stuck up here?
                              No food? Only cloud-juice to drink?
Well, says Coyote
     I told you
     I di'n't work that out yet
he never does
he always gets himself stuck some kind of a place

& I says
          How you get up here?
& he says
           Well, I looked up & thought it'd be nice
& Swoosh! here I was
           same with you, eh?

OK, I says
     I really wish we was back down

& O boy
    all of a sudden we're going down real fast
         pretty soon them mountains & lake
                  they ain't so far away
                  coming up faaast...
Coyote, I says
          how we gonna stop?
I di'n't work that out either
says Coyote
     he never does
lake or mountains I says
               we're gonna make an awful big splash
& they're coming up real fast & near
& lots of sharp rocks
& I just don't like that
                 it's no good

but I shouts out
           STOP
& just like that, we stops
        about half my height above the beach pebbles
     & then just fall
            me on my arse
          & Coyote on his nose
  not great but we ain't even near dead

Hooh! says Coyote
        you're good at that
Never again, says I
& off we goes

But still I wonder at what it looked like
                up in those clouds.

Cut Foot & Midnight
1/6/08

To my Departed Wife

Your humanity called you to distant kin
You left & the birds soon followed
The days fell with the Autumn leaves
Winter brings its own darkness & chill
Snow & thaw, snow & thaw again
Frost-bound branches can't stir to speak
Slick ice stays stubbornly settled
Waves push the wind north or south
Then turn to push it south or north
Mountains veil themselves with wandering mists
Other mists wipe the lake from sight
With you beyond mountains & rivers
Breaks in the sky are somehow less blue
Though ice makes the path dangerous
I watch buds swelling just a bit
Spring may return from the South one day
Something has chosen me to speak in Winter
In the Eastern Capital, loyal ministers sleep
Elders & children scorned while the empire rots
Hungry beggars haunt the busy streets
The hungry Emperor cherishes his friends with gold
They praise soldiers & weapons loudly
Somewhere people die in mindless war
Better to drink tea in the lakeside hut
Away here in lofty mountain spaces
I need greens for a simple meal
Water in the creek never flows the same

Yueh-fu: a Chinese form developed from ballad style: 5 characters per line; the italicized lines are borrowed from two Chinese Tang & Sung poets.
1/2/11

Drinking Tea In the Mountains

I recall former times & places
Island town officials heap laws
River city merchants heap cash
Here, clouds hide the East mountains
Late snow falls, mountain snow
Early geese delay their northern journey
Soft waves caress the stony shore
Drink tea & watch the early moon.

Lu-shih
a Chinese form: 5 characters per each of eight lines

29/3/05

May Morning

Dark clouds this late spring morning
The front range blue-green & pale green
Mount Loki cloaked in snow
Here birches, firs stir small wind
Wind follows waves on Kootenay Lake
I stand at the window watching
Drink tea slowly, step outside
Wind, waves, distant stream singing

Lu-shih
27/5/10

Dry Now

Birch twig an Autumn wind dropped
a twiglet, two buds, brown & dead
in the Capital, they scold away all the scholars
bandits remain to grasp fiercely at the Empire

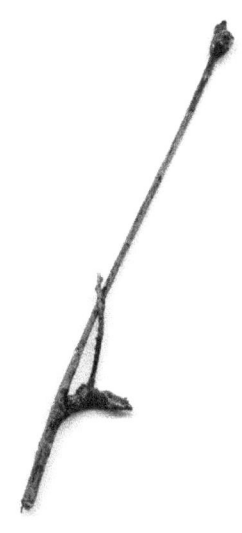

for Sung Po-jen
who made the first art book ever in 1278: Guide to Capturing a Plum
Blossom
one hundred ink sketches & poems on plum blossoms & Yuan politics.
I follow his form: 5 characters for each of four lines

13/9/12

Late Snow

Far, far from the Middle Realm
new dragon boats search these waves
yet Ch'u Yuan's long gone
gone with the weeping Phoenix
& the Ch'i-lin sickens & limps away

Our ruler keeps his court leashed tight
& heaps sacrifices to greed & anger
his boot pressing the land & people

When it's autumn, cling to summer
when it's spring, bid winter farewell
this late chill shocks hopeful buds
late flakes sting my face sharply
spring is a faint & doubtful memory

The Master said:
Good ones love mountains
Wise ones love water

Yueh-fu
The Master is Master K'ung-fu Tse, Confucius
This citation is from the Analects, Bk VI, # 21
The Phoenix (Feng) appears only in times of peace & prosperity
The Ch'i-lin ('Unicorn') is seen only when a benevolent ruler or great sage appears
The story: Ch'u Yuan's counsel to the king he advised, Chinshiang of Chu was neglected, & Shen state fell into ruin. Ch'u Yuan drowned himself in the Yellow River, & it is said that the Dragon Boats still search for him.....

24/2/12

II. Time:
Astrology

   First folk
O we turned our eyes
          to the stars
     gave them names
   & counted moons & festivals

   For the Planets our cousins
we found names of power
           to us mighty, primal, willful,
               beyond understanding
   we say they move us still
        shall it be Mars
              for blood & iron
        Venus
            for wine & roses

             Jupiter's unyielding will
            or Saturn's lead
                    & mastery of Time?

  & the moon our neighbour & sister
                as a shepherdess
             leads tides
                  migrating birds perhaps
               & who knows what else
      they follow the subtle pulse of her varying drum

  & further far
    we said & say
            the names of the Galaxy
                             turning slow
                       scatter their own influence
                         across the night
                      Lion & Ram
                        Archer & Water-maiden
          & the dancing Twins

                   & others named & unnamed
                             distill starry destinies
                    & the Pleiades bring rain

How this might be
     I cannot say
   but I know this
           on a clear December night
        I felt the Moon's heat
            though but her memory
                                  of the Sun
         it warmed my hands
               my face
                    & spirit most of all

Close to the Sun
    is fiery death
even here
    the skin may burn

The hard forces of the stars
        we could not bear close by
        grow mild with distance
their true & subtler virtues
            whose image is light
            remain unchecked
        they reach us here
         & greet our eyes & steps
              with grace & power

    From lifetimes away
we gaze upon them
    with unshielded eyes

The 1885 engraving is a brilliant montage of motifs from previous centuries & in various techniques. It was designed for Camille Flammarion's 1888 L'atmosphere: populaire meteorologie.

7,14,22/4/14

III. People

Baker Electric

Wabi
    perhaps
    the pang of a perfect instant

When I was a child
        in Oak Bay
        in Victoria
Oh, 60, 70 years ago
two old ladies
    old, very old
        sisters, I must think
            as pale as parchment lilies
        & wore black
            always
        & great black Edwardian bonnets with veils
they had decided what was good
    & stuck with it

I saw them only rarely
how did I know they were the *same* old ladies?
    because I saw them in their car
              a 1911 Baker Electric
                    Opera Coupe
a grand Art Nouveau thing
    taller than it was wide
   & almost than it was long
     with bevelled quarter lights
       a hardwood tiller mounted with brass
         to steer it by
 & on the door pillar
   a cut-glass flower vase
      with always a white blossom
        for the black paint
           always shining
            despite the crackles of age
there was only room for 2 or 3
            sitting against the padded back
 & it was dead silent
       only the tyres rustled on the road

I'm telling all this
   because it helps you to understand what's coming

About 1946 in the afternoon
   I stood at the Bus Stop
      on the SouthEast side
         of Oak Bay Avenue & Richmond road

A boy between 8 & 10
   came rattling his bicycle down the Avenue
      weaving rapidly from side to side
         like a mad rabbit

    & then came the ancient ladies in their Baker Electric
               silent as a night cloud
    & when they were just passing that oblivious cyclist
               honked an unbelievably loud & noxious horn
    the boy fell off his bike
    & the last I saw of the old ladies then
               they were bending & bucking over the tiller
                    laughing like crows

Long gone now
    ancient ladies & equally ancient car
        save in my odd memory

Mais ou sont les neiges d'antan?

The final line: 'but where are the snows of years gone by?' is borrowed from Francois Villon's elegiac villanelle, Ballade des dames du temps jadis, on departed beautiful ladies

28/8/14

Terrible Ted

When my artist friend DDan still lived
                         he told me about Terrible Ted
                                  who gave him his name:
                     Dangerous Dan

Terrible Ted had been a TV wrestler
     when he retired to Kaslo village in the 1980's
        & he & DDan got on famously
                               as two scallywags will
       Ted taught DDan how to mock-fight
              a useful TV Wrestlers' skill

               For several years
Terrible Ted lived with Brownie
                      who happened to be a bear
                          goodnatured & charming
& when Ted was off in town
      Brownie stayed on his chain
              by the little house
               toward Kaslo Back Road

So one night
         Brownie safely at home
Terrible Ted went to the pub
      he came back up the dirt road behind the Golf Course
      then crossed a fairway
          when he saw Brownie toddling across the grass
'Brownie!
      How did you get loose?
                         Come here!'
Brownie said nothing
So Ted got him by the neck scruff
           despite some grumbling

      & dragged him home
                to where
                          still patiently waiting on his chain
                          was Brownie.
Ted let the other one go
    'Neighbour! I had someone else's bear!'

Remember the mock fighting?
sometimes on a hot summer day
       & Kaslo full of tourists
          having seen a likely bunch of innocents
Ted & Ddan would meet on Front Street
       bump into each other & pick a fearsome fight
       yelling, punching, groaning
       swinging wildly
       grasping, struggling & breaking loose

& when it was clear that one at least
                 of the tourists
                      who had been standing
                shocked & stunned
                      by that terrific row
              woke up enough to start off for help
Ted & DDan rolled into the gutter
      rolled apart
      leapt up
    then dusted each other off
      shook hands & shouted
                  'Thanks, Friend;
                  I needed that!'
& wandered off their carefully separate ways
        secretly glancing back
                  to judge the effect
The good old days
         aren't really so far off   *19/5/15*

IV. Beasts
Bear

At the start of the trail to Fletcher Falls
Misty the Dog
    wrought up
    running ahead &
        whuffling
            after the scent of something
 then gave it up & went off down the trail

    I follow
& then see
        about 7 metres down the bank to the right
        a bear with butternut fur
            strolling through brush
            has paused to look at me
It's become my habit
        when I meet a beast
            to stop & speak

            Good Day. I'm glad to see you
            You look well, & you're beautiful;
            Come by again some time

& the bear simply looked on mildly
        & listened
then we both moved along at our ease
        like two people
          pleased to have met each other
        & wishing each other well
        or distant family chance met

Well enough
    but there's more

I look into the forest
       into which the bear has disappeared
       at the trees, shrubs, little plants
         the stones along the rail
       & the sky above
& wonder yet again
         how large my family might be.

18/6, 14/7/15

Otter

    This quiet afternoon
I sit on the Thinking Rock
    just north of the Fletcher Creek mouth
& gaze unthinking
       at Kootenay lake
       at the silent, enormous sky
    & the peaks & ranges of the high Purcells
& sink into that silence

Something I can't recall catches my mind
       perhaps a quick movement seen from the corner of the eye
       perhaps a small sound that nearly misses the ear
I look down to the shore four metres below
        where a big otter silently arrived
           dace in its jaws
         & lies on a broad stone to eat

    I watch while the fish goes inside & down
then make a quiet sound
the otter looks up for a long moment
        slides into the water
        silent & smooth away
                no fuss at all

& I look up to the mountains again
& listen intently to the silence

10, 29/5/13

Carried Away

It comes to me suddenly
that the cats & dog
                curled at rest
are small gods
    proper to this household
                 entire in themselves
            & wrapped in single light

How can one not honour them?

& these other beasts
                recently met
  the little bear cub
                clinging to a tree

at the height of my eyes

& the doe
  who gleans the bruised apples fallen under my tree
      her eyes large to see
      her ears turning
             scanning everywhere

How can I not honour them?

There are trees
        I cannot think of but as my friends
& one day
        this mountain
                will tell me its true name

21/8/15

Anne Heard

Kaslo Community Garden

The old village water cistern
unused, a safety hazard
deep and filling with water and debris
To reduce risk filled with excellent drainage
gravel and round river rock rubble
You still see rims of concrete edges of the cistern basin
Pieces of concrete appear in unexpected places
The soil is not deep enough
to bury all evidence of former purpose
Today the lot is a community garden
a repurposing to reclaim land
The Village property is lease provided and supported
mission and goals agreed, executive governs
Allotments are assigned to
members, school participants
community food cupboard
help yourself gardens
Soil is not deep enough to avoid the rock
As shovels turn, stones are picked, piled, carried
accumulate in a ditch on an outside corner of the garden
Endless wealth used as markers
to outline the edge of a garden
and weigh in as anchors
Gardeners dream of deep soil as they pile on straw
compost, plant green crops and work in leaves
Soil to bury the rock and gravel tub
Soil to grow food and community

Brassica

Oh, the delectable cabbage family, brassica, we hail
broccoli
rutabaga
brussel sprouts
cauliflower
rapini
kale
Diners prefer the green nutty bitter sweet crunch
Growers decry the pests that hasten forth and munch
Myriad insects loiter in leaf litter, emerge, take possession
flea beetle
aphid
caterpillar
cabbage moth
harlequin beetle
a procession
Foraging in spring, to satisfy appetites
fuelling reproductive succession
Gardeners defend the organic crops with aggression
nasturtium
marigolds
diatomaceous earth
fight the good fight
Water and earth nutrients, sun provides light
Young plants are coddled and covered
strong sturdy survivors
to be human providers

Spring Along The Fraser

The river sweepers rear and bounce
flow slapping
High water rules, washing soil away down stream
Roots eroded
Trees surrender to gravity
Watch them lean and sway
their underpinnings loosing ground
Bowed long trunks
branches
bent arbours sweep across the water mirror
The dance reflects around fast flow
Weighty dunking current runs the gauntlet
Snags recoil, erupt
spring back, whack
danger lurks to rise and crack
Trunks bent in sweeping curves
piling into tangled jams
Trapped, current tows the undermined flotilla
to meet the outside curve
Sweepers float
flounce bounce, submerge and rise
stripped by water's force, roots exposed
Tree skeletons
white twisted boneyard
uncrossable interlocked guard
River passage through rocks and silty mud
await the season's flood that frees
swish whistle thud
Steer clear of underwater trees

Haiku Along the Way

Painted Turtles log
soaking in the warmth of sun
at the sewage bog

Be still, and listen
stand or sit and contemplate
Observe life hasten

Balsam root blossom
cling sun-drenched on steep dry slopes
yellow heads beg come

Vivid moss cushion
soft green feather reaching fronds
finding spring's potion

High beyond our reach
mountain gold upon slopes glow
wind spills wealth on us

To Carlyle Mountain Lodge

We meet our hiking party at Kaslo Community Garden
ready with food, clothes, sleeping bags
Prepared to test our strength, to be with the land
adults and children together

Convoy to Sandon, on highway 31A
now slowing
now shifting into back road gear
Four wheel drive maneuvers the shoulder of the mountain
Skillful drivers carefully negotiating
staying on track
passengers peering over cliff edge
An old forestry road
scoured rocky rutted tracks
Hold on
Negotiate deep water bars
Safely at the parking lot, turn around facing the return trip
Make room for the next vehicle
Park tight to fit

Unload, hoist packs, begin up a trail
simple well laid out
trapper and miner blazed
Artifacts make historic notes along the path
leg hold traps fused shut with rust, shovels, an axe handle
A log cabin standing, door open
the roof open to the elements, windows with no glass
Inside, as if the trapper just walked out, thinking to return
bottles half full of yellow liquid
What could it be
Pots and pans lay about
bent out of shape, hanging on a nail
Children and adults investigate and wonder

A lunch stop at Sweet Lake invites rest
Children excited to swim turn into waders
they step into frigid water, a soak for hot feet
We mark the end of easy walking
The trail heads up long steep switch backs
uneven soft ground, loose rocks roll underfoot
Trail scrubbed through an avalanche path
pearly everlastings along angular grey stone
Watch the footing, keep on moving
gasp for breath, pay attention
Up to the next traverse
Stop at a mountain fountain stream to fill water bottles
catch a breather, look down where we have come from
Below, a narrow line runs back and forth up the steep approach
following a passable zigzag angle
Hidden from view in turns
the path disappears, behind rock, and foliage
to reappear on our sight line

Who built this trail, considerate of those to come
Eyes lift to take the next step
We walk along a packed wide trail built for horses
lugging ore from the "Mountain Con Silver Mine"
A short side trip to the entrance finds rail tracks in place
Entrance still fully framed and sturdy
allows cautious steps into the dark
Points of interest grab our attention
mining tools, hardware, debris abounds
Children pick through solid metal concentrator crusher balls
rough rusting pipes and rails
Treasure to imagine when it was an active mine
All is left in place, a found museum

Who were these hard rock miners
How did they endure the endless work, the isolation

What dreams drove the search for their Eldorado
Dave tells the story of three miners
working into November
caught in an avalanche
One killed outright
One injured, legs useless
One unscathed to go for help, never to arrive or to return
The injured man, snowshoes on hands
made it to Cody, pulling himself along the snow
Over rough terrain he did it
Tough guy
I wonder what life had in store for him next

We shudder at the real life drama
Proceed up through a rock slide of 1910
The mountain gave way, granite shearing
break away boulders, roaring, shaking the world
rumbling, tumbling, rolling down the slope
a geologic shift, a catastrophic difference

We balance across tossed boulders to find the path again
Weary of the climb
we see the top
feel relief coming to the ridge
Look down, ease our breath
take in the view over the col

Descend to stroll the drop to Carlyle Mountain Lodge
recognizing the twin peaks of Mount Carlyle
Follow flagged track along mossed, lichened jutting boulders
heather softened alpine streams
I bring up the rear in slow measure steps
By the time I arrive children are playing on the deck
their energy restored on arrival

To Meadow Mountain

Sky blue, from horizons to valley floor
forecast prediction high 30 degrees Celsius or more
September peaks exhibit larch touched green golden hue
Steady resting steps lift to rewards of glacial view

Gaining altitude, ears pop, temperature changes
Shade and breeze cools, sun heat soars, temperature ranges
Still, glaciers melt, there is no new snow
We pause to drink it in, take in the slow

Waterfalls sound revelling, tumbling mirth
frothing sliding fountains, slipping curtains over rocky earth
Serenity Mountain is foremost in eye's mind
Quibble and Squabble peaks, arguments left behind

Snow Melt

Spring is in the valley summoning its verdant takeover
Snow in high places slips, unloading from the bottom of the pack
Sliding melt water, pouring, spitting off ledges
Skidding, falling over sweeping precipice and rock face
seeping into moss beds

The enchanted flounder prince left a streak of blood

Do you wish for nothing — are you well content
Hear the folktale message to discover what is meant
A flounder prince's streak of blood sinks to the ocean floor
The fisherman's wife always wanted more and more

Hear the folktale's message to discover what is meant
A hunger for life yearns to have all the riches in the land
A flounder prince's streak of blood sinks to the ocean floor
Pay the price —wealth, possessions, power— are really only lent

A hunger for life yearns to have all the riches in the land
Life's best rewards are reliably in our mind and hand
Pay the price —wealth, possessions, power— are really only lent
The riches of our culture spring from family and friend

Life's best rewards are reliably in our mind and hand
A flounder prince's streak of blood sinks to the ocean floor
Pay the price —wealth, possessions, power— are really only lent
Do you wish for nothing, are you well content

Comfort Confab

I am dreaming
you and I sit on swings suspended in foggy air
We can't see the sky or the ground, all is a cloud
We see each other,
The swings, thick long planks, holes drilled in the ends
Thick long ropes strung through the boards
tied with large strong knots
suspend us from a sky hook somewhere
We gently swing and talk about comfort
Eventually our bottoms hurt
feeling the hard plank, we complain
Instantly swings disappear
replaced by adirondack garden chairs supporting us
I sit far back, my seat at the back of the chair
my back up against the chair back
arms resting on the wide arms of the chair
You perch at the front of the chair
 I counsel, "Relax, slide to the back, be comfortable"
We laugh
A friend walks by
Observing us she remarks
"If you want comfort you should try the new chair
It is a limited edition guaranteed most comfortable chair ever
It is too bad it is not available
You will have to wait for the next edition to be comfortable"

We both want one

A Hot Day in Cold Water

Wipe the sweat from my brow
Cool me down
Keep me cool
Wade into cold water
Where all is well

My body registers and takes time
Adjust the thermostat, submerge
Gasp and shudder
Reassure, this is okay
Collect the chill and swim
It is good for the heart

Feel the comfort of buoyant float
Momentum of the stroke
Efficient practised power
Smooth rhythmic breath
Cool and collected

Speak Easy

Words with wisdom and purpose sound
love displays, however short
We define romance sport
by ordinary tributes bound

Along our loving path of landscape tolls
we stroll to find our way to mutual goals
Thoughtful responses seek
to think before we speak

He is waiting patiently outside for me

Is it important that he is patient or is it that he waits
that he never lets me down
that he is seldom late
His face calm, not a scowl or frown
I depend on him to wait for me to be
ready and want to go with me

When I walk out the door
I look for him to meet my eyes
to feel the lift of belonging gauge
translate our silent language
Between us there, together flies
"Let's go home, as we have done before"

Sheila Murray-Nellis

The Wolf

Sleeping by the open window
I awake to the bark
then the liquid howl
of the leggy wolf
who lifts his snout
to the wind's ladder.

He stands in the deep snow
asking his question
then listens in the moonlight
for the answer.

They are far off now —
why has he lingered,
whose voice wrapped him in
scarves of light
while the pack jauntily trotted
over the wooded path?

Holding back
has emptied
the hollow in his heart
now filled with
more longing
than he can contain.

We hear it
as curdled notes
rise
through the silver
and bounce
off the high peaks.

Wolf Cull

No song erupting from the silence,
Slick howl to jolt and lick our spine,
With all the shock of violence,
We hear instead the copter whine.

Slick howl to jolt and lick our spine
When wolves pass through the winter snow,
We hear instead the copter whine,
The caribou population low

When wolves pass through the winter snow
Over trails the snowmobilers make —
The caribou population low,
Culling's for the animals' sake.

Over the trails snowmobilers make
The killing is easier than nature intended.
Culling for the animals' sake
Will keep the playing ground well tended.

The killing easier than nature intended,
The weapons more deadly than tooth and claw
Will keep the playing ground well tended,
A balance maintained, choking awe.

The weapons more deadly than tooth and claw
With all the shock of violence,
A balance maintained by choking awe
From song to slaughter, then to silence.

Invisible Highway

The moose traveled the same invisible highway
we saw the buck deer go:

First the splash
then antlers bobbing above the waves;

the frigid lake buoys them
to the far shore where they scramble

onto the pebble beach by Clute Creek,
pick their way through the cedars

where the logging road leads up
to St. Mary's Wilderness Park.

It's the same route every time.

I step into my boat,
the lake slick, then stirred.

Already I drift
from the dock, the cliffs
stark, sheer to the bottom,

this pallet of doubt
my door.

I'm here where others
have gone before

through lashing waters
that churn and masticate.

Across the lake
a voice parts the waves

breathes through
wind and thrashing hooves
and I come to the shore

where wilderness leads to the core
on high and windy mountains.

I listen: the ice melts
above the sprouting meadows
and its trickle
overflows the tarn.

The Flying Lesson

On the porch I hold a basket of wash
I will pin to the line;
my eyes scan the pine
where the barred owl roosts.

Perched on the back of the lawn chair,
a young owlet, fully grown
but with voice not yet honed,
barks to his mother's hoots;

for ten minutes I freeze
in the plea of this open space,
a mother's verbal embrace
apart from bumps of trees;

despite owlet protest, she
urges him on, pleads him to try
at still of dusk, the nest nearby,
his wings are full and sleek and strong.

Suddenly the young one's wings unfold;
he lifts, circling the yard
on gray wings newly barred,
swerves into the shadows alone.

Autumn Poems

I.

Raw onset of cold
gold leaves spin
low clouds
pinch and shiver.

You leave your twigs
reluctantly
trembling
I know what you mean
I, too, want to stay connected,

but then you let go
you lift and twirl.

II.

Trees, why do you throw
away your gold?

Why rattle your coins
against my window?

Why these leaves face down in mud,
your naked trunk contorted
swaying with breath?

III.

And then I gave away my gold,
said the oak.

I gave the ravens my smile,
splashed joy at the wind,

undid the knots in the leaves,
took off my cloak,

and flapped fear like sheets
in sunshine.

Now naked,
I lift my woody arms

and am clothed
in a white gown.

While Alone, Thoughts Escape

The sky is mulling over its thoughts.

She has more teeth than she needs for chewing;
her lips struggle to keep them in;
their yellow bite drains the white
of her eyes and muddies the grey roots
of her hair. Somewhere she has set
her glasses — if only she could remember
if only she could focus her mind:
this kind of trouble becomes more familiar;
it would be funny except for the wasted time.

Her thoughts are over the sky, mulling.

She spirals up the logging road,
paintbrush blush on the banks, black
spruce needle the mountain's back.
Up here trees sift the wind,
raven wing feathers whine in reply;
a creek bubbles over stones,
fists of clouds loosen
then make shadow puppets
on the hill's screen.

See where the mountain gave way,
tumbled in a mess of stones, and how
the moss reclaims it for the trees.

She reclaims her thoughts tumbling
over and under the clouds
like cumulus that darken,
become nimbus,
roll with rumbling,

spark with light, bright
thoughts with darker underbellies,
dark thoughts that crack
their shells and drop their raw suns
into the bowl the hills make.

Bear

Beyond the kitchen window, a black bear, plump
and handsome, fur sleek
in the morning light:

A bumper crop of huckleberries
on the mountainside
kept him busy through September.

Now he sniffs the fruit trees by the house,
and finds them picked clean.
Grape vines by my window stripped of all

but the yellow leaves, translucent on the vine.
He's on his back legs, nostrils flaring.
The generator I put on

for the laundry disturbs him.
Even without my apples and grapes
His rump fat ripples as he runs.

I sometimes, too, fail to notice
how full I have become,
see just the empty trees.

An Ebb and Flow and Then We Break Through

Where the tide is lowest, there it rises highest,
the almost forgotten place, the core

where waves in watery clench, collapse,
drag long fingers through the pebbles,
a place forgotten almost, missed;

the year whose waves roll one on another,
foam and spittle, rake and suck on stone,
tumbling moments, one spilling into the next
as if not to forget

how high at each apex we travel, and then
the death of everything, then this — the impossible
break through of clear eyed eternity;
how quickly, then, the descent into sleep,

how quickly the year returns and our breath catches
when brightness blasts from black night
more than we can take in;

Later — cottonwood leaves shining,
birch leaves shining,
speaking when the breeze lifts
undulating daisies, each buttoned with the sun;

bees in purple clover lift and dip,
their buzz zips the air closed,
now open,

and our lids unfold with fingers — oh
so gentle — of light

right now, while we sit facing each other,
listening to the varied thrush among the spruce,
the wind ruffling the grasses,
touching first your cheek,
then mine.

To You Who Lives There Now

Have you taken the path yet
out past the house
and over the ledge on the north side
               of the barn
where the mother killdeer feigns a broken
wing to lure you from her little brown eggs
               laid in a cup of rock?
Go through the gate on the broken rail fence
               overgrown with hawthorn
along the grassy trail, past boulders
into the green lace of cedar branches.
Squirrels will chitter a warning as you approach —
               Ignore that.
Veer to the right and you will come
to the spongy moss speckled red
               open to the sky.
Cedars huddle around the edges.
Fall on your face there —
               listen
to what the breeze says.
You are meant to bear
that kind of light.

Conversation

In the kitchen
a bee bumping against the glass,

a spill of black pepper,

words unspoken to spare pain,
silences between parent and child,
protection and counter-protection,
a knowing and avoidance;

robin slamming the window
against an imaginary rival —
to know, to really know
the myriad ways we fall

and still to get up each day,
to rise between the moon's silver
and the blowing in of clouds,
to await the healing rain on the cracking soil.

Through Darkness the Hidden Beauty Rises

Spongy moss, luminescent,
hugs boulders and fallen trees;
here and there
in the humus
forgotten squirrel stashes
send up sprouts;

from elsewhere the dappled motion
as a breeze fingers the upper branches.

But in this stillness nothing is still:
the earth rolls towards darkness,
and after a sleepless night
we notice the glow at the horizon
and the leakage of purplish light
as the first rays skitter across the low grass;

between silhouetted mountains,
distant peaks, clothed in light,
are skirted with cloud;
we are clothed with what we become,
a beauty that covers our lack.

This is what we know: the loss
that bends through the dark towards the light,
the constant motion hurling us along.
We are part of that dance from the depths
of the molecules that form us,
the vibrations we make even when we stand still
listening to the music we become.

Whatever brokenness brought on this suffering,
Whatever meaninglessness or unwelcome surprise,
the pain carries with it a key to unlock a spaciousness
always there but now in relief, leaning against the glass.

You will become this window, this dead
wood and fitted glass with blinds shut tight
or stripped clear and shining the distant light.

Robert Banks Foster

Crocus

What
        we know of flowers
no doubt we could
        measure
        talk ourselves silly
tell which scent was in the house
        when we were born

and meadows
        disguised as fields of the dead
ancient lettering
        while
spring is the land of orange flowers

Though prairie crocus blossomed late this year
in our own time we caught it opening

I don't know all names for colour and root
        though I've seen petals through my life
I remember putting
        cold bulbs in the earth

but I've come this far into spring

        uncovering you
        finding flowers

Water Sequence

"Water is the healing place." Maud Barlow

I.

1.

We lose the stream
and about a billion people around the world routinely
drink un-
healthy water.
Holding to life by our fingertips
facing each other without water
water "privatization" is a global experiment.
Ice is the foundation of lives.
Blowing high cloud below the moon
I could not sleep for the song.
Old roots melt snow drinking first
the golden ripple dollars.
The corporate state has nothing to offer but fear.
But indeed I am mostly water
rainbow's end,
water running down amid the rising land.
Though there is water inside
and the sea is here now,
the steady barrage of illusions
and what is outside you
sells your life.
Resource war in the 21st century.
A lot of people have lost confidence in the water itself.
Santa Claus, a man with a whip, **"Here, have a drink."**

2.

It all goes into the clouds.
We don't get to the unknown spring.
Drinking the ocean, sliding on the ocean
in and out in my childhood
identity now through products
all end up in the ocean
trading in these rights to pollute
every rain spout tied to the water works
unable to see our reflections.

3.

Faith in the marketplace replaces many faiths.
All tears collected — the rushing river hits the rocks.
BP and Shell had meetings with government officials
in the run-up to the invasion of Iraq.
The rain on the roof sold back to you.
Water lensing the stones it covers flowing.
Clouds above and below the shore.
Faith in the marketplace replaces many faiths.

II.

1.

If water were ours to do with what we will.
Grassroots, coalface, and fence line struggles
facing each other without water
reflect the gap in the mountains
that grief and shame will always disturb
depths of pond and stream.
The water in bodies collected, distilled, and bottled.

2.

I wake at dawn set up for dictatorship.
Two rainbows or two reflections side by side
are banished as heretics . . .
though ice is the foundation of their lives.
Leave fossil fuels in the ground.

Oil troubles the living stream
waiting for heat to come more than heat this is.
Water inside
rain inside the valley coming at us
comforts in the night.
All the dawn red snow in water
courses in my mother's dreams of drowning
that there was nothing to be done.
We lose the stream unless all drops gather.

Nevertheless, the difference between
what is inside you giving life
and water as the healing place
and what is outside you stealing your life
all ends up in the ocean.

Water is the healing place.

Eschatology

They went to all the proper clinics.
They took at the right approaches
to reach the perfect moment just one time.

They mastered Masters and johnsoned Johnson
till old at twenty-three or thirty-nine
amid collapse, from an accidental ease
their orgasms occurred together, exactly once.

Ecstatic, though almost on crutches, from
what makes beggars limp and scholars dunces,
they published it in papers, they telephoned
their friends. Praise ringing in their skulls
they crawled to bed again.

They still lie there. They died in lying
and wait forever the second coming.

Finally

Lust burns and
makes a landscape
of its own. Peace
I'm told
is another
place. Healing
is the other art.
But I do not think
two fires from Heaven fight.

Dionysus and St. Peter
both once knew
       we live by fire.

Body on body
line on line
hand touching hand
healing calm:
the end of war—

what bodies do
or may not do despite
the howling to make things
simple and safe—

is looking at each other from the flames
plainly in the face.

For George
(d. November 24, 1993)

By the Old Stone Church, by the graves of Asham's children—
>*He gave,*
>*He took,*
>*He will restore.*
>*He doeth*
>*all things well.*

With you beside me in the old red Datsun at 35 below
I get out, change as fast as I can into my new Canadian
       Tire snowmobile suit
and come back in from the cold.

Across the Red River, north east far as the road goes,
where Chief Peguis camped first on this flood plain
finding villages dead from typhoid,
the delta ice is feet thick—
unquestionable solidity to the horizon.

We walk out on the sea of glass in Revelations.
We walk out until the islands hide the shore
and then go back to whatever seemed
warm life in Winnipeg.

But now you go on,
your black Greek sailor's cop and scarf,
frost on your beard,
across the wider ice
past the old Saulteaux fishing camp
to the lake itself.

You go into the north.
Air blurs your passage.

Trapped in the Story

We are all taught
to despise animals.
Only, sometimes I want
to be your Bête.
Animals remind us of
the parts despised for being bestial,
beast within blood.
I lumber round the rooms. Occasionally
you like the passion of bear
but fear the way he takes his meat
or lifts his ears at wildness in the wood.

For all your hatred of the words
part of you still
wants to be clean and pure, wants me
to be Prince Charming done in marble
kindly father, not human
nor breathing, with no darkness
to disturb your places of pure light.

Funny. You, Beauty, accuse
me of using reason, when the power
of passivity cold as a china plate
shows to me your geometric mind.
Is it my mother in you that I hate—
always accusing my father's anger,
always winning with the rational knife
the rituals below the castle kitchen?

It is too late
for me to go back now; the beast was fixed
upon my head at three years old.
These last six months when I've seen it in the mirror

I have begun to say
a glance at it is good.
Again and again you tell me tiredly each night
how I scare you, then sometimes
say also that you love. I lumber round the rooms.
I growl and starve and stare. Sometimes
I get more hope from my reflection.
I want to stop
our circling of each other.
Why will you not kiss me? I must
go out soon
and kill beyond these walls. Who
ultimately shining would it offend
if actually you lived, asked me to live?

Glacial Going

For Kiara Lynch and all the Jumbo Requiem people
With thanks to Douglas Noblet for photographs of ice

With quotations from Andrew Marvel, Aeschylus, William
Dunbar, & John Ralston Saul

1.

Chunks fall.
Water denied.

It's only
ice into the sea.

Divide the world
in geometric lines.
Exclusion from the body.

Who but Riel stood on surveyors chains?

Glacial
Slow

Glacial
Slow

Summer's lease hath all too short a date

but summer stays.

Time knew once
the flow was slow.
How much suffering must melt before

Wisdom falling to the heart
teaches moderation of our lives.

They have all gone away
Timor mortis conturbat me.

2.

The glacial tongue leaves a lake.

Ice faces vanish into the faces of the rocks.

We think of ice as cold as if the word we use for people applies to it.

Once to welcome the other was about respect.

Water denied
leaves only rock faces.

Water affirmed
is our skin.

3.

Ice goes away.
Timor mortis conturbat me.

Look at the world's north ice:

1980 looks like a goat face with a body bloated out of its mind. 2009, like a skinny trapper with a dwindling pack.

Yet it is only human to meet faces in the glacier's edge
falling into the sea.

Other is
zombies, vampires, the dark house,
the dwellings that look like infinite squares of desert.

Yep, that face looks like a screaming skull.
Claw marks.
A dead snowman's head rolling down.
The odd dignified rational 18th century profile,
a wise native man, and a great King Kong resting.

Arches through ice.

Great rivers vanishing.
Methane beginning to kill the world in 20 years.

And that benign face
I used to see out my door.

4.

A horn at the glacier's edge.

If glaciers are cold as metaphor
why the joy at requiem?

Begin again.

Drums on the mountain shake.

Hamlet

The house quiets. I enter,
and pausing in the wings, try
to catch clues in the echoes
of what's next—my life in this age.

Night points darkness at me
through a thousand opera glasses.
Abba, Father, if you can
take this cup away.

I love how You've persisted with your plan.
I'm still willing to play my part.
But now another plot is going on.
I want out.

Yet the acts go on
finding their way to just one end.
I am alone. Pharisees drown everything.
"Life is not a walk across a field."

Boris Pasternak, trans. Robert Banks Foster

Up

(why up)
along the lake
north though going east
then truly north
where arms of water join
under the sight of Toad Rock
clinging to the walls of Coffee Creek

the road clings
we cling to the road
the avalanche of ourselves
the memories of ourselves
once the dirt road or the gravel road
when my father travelled here
seeking diseased plants to heal

he took the boat
but drove
in later years
when I was six
and he told me of the up and down
cliffs that entered my nights.

Awake from the bowl of night
The sleep the government lends to its music
The sleep appearance lends to its music
The sleep money lends to its music

opiate doze snoring, stupor
sleep without dreams

The cosmeticians who teach us imperfection so they
can perfect us.
We belong to the land.
We are told to rape our mother.

Henry Moore at the A. G. O.

Shapes look through my vertebrae.
I walk round. With me they discuss
polished bone. Perhaps I have done this
a dozen times. They're never
what I remember. In their ancestry
stone endures.

Each light is different.
I've come to this room
through the end of a marriage, loves
and unfaithfulness, madness
and a new home in the world.

Though bronze was the sculptor's destination,
these plaster casts converse with stone and bone.

In fields, junk yards, along beaches, throughout life
we pick up pieces like these—pebbles, driftwood,
parts broken in the sea, what's left
of an animal—that lives in us—
something we only know we're seeking when it comes into
our hands.

Part is memory. When did the moon through curtains
show her knee or mine just so? How long back through fossil
seas
have these shapes swayed? But something else occurs. Not
only are they
made, but they are
to carry us forward, bring our whole bodies through each
shadow.
Stone, bone, and even bronze flesh
give birth and teach more than what was.

In their talk
it is possible to
know yourself enough to see
that the face emerging from the wall
is not hope or fear
but vision inquiring on its own.

In their company instep and heel
footprint on a path
that goes its way on its own.
By their direction they
articulate the end of life
marrow in the bone, centre
travelling.

Just to Let You Know

Blue newborn Picasso
made no sound.
Don Salvatore, uncle and doctor
blew cigar smoke into Picasso's face.
His talent all his life—
he screamed.

The watermelon at lunch sliced in wedges
eaten or uneaten
looked like ships on a white shore
England or perhaps Troy.
Blood diluted, the only desert green
great ships in the desert
arching over us, seedless.

Death a national spectacle
the minotaur
long live death
dry run bombs in the Prado.

Language is what hasn't happened yet
let's not romanticize the product
over 5000 bombs
do it because you can
the language ready for prophecy
death makes night the afternoon
history a cry in the street
anticipates the eyes of Dora Mar.

At the MOMA a long time ago
Get off the elevator
look at Guernica
I didn't expect it
No one expects Guernica.

Ancient as stigmata
no that's too sanctified
ancient as nails pounded into hands
a body suspended from two nails
carried, an image against the wars of Charlemagne
to show what he was doing.

Horses scream.

Sheila Falle

Mind Fields

In Spring who wonders
About the message
I believe it begins
Like a memory
On a dark night
Riddled by stars

Someone once said
With all due gravity
Are we there yet?

Yes, fear not
Celebrate together

I Believe

Rhymes that wind inside the mind
like the tangle of a too long nightgown
awaken

It Begins

Little in a little house
The wide world waits outside
for us to hear the magic
that in sounds around us hides
Incantations swirl about
Lullabies and nursery rhymes
Good morning and Good night
One day we awaken
Saying our first words
With words we explore everywhere
Naming, claiming, aiming dares
As every word has meaning
We think all else should too
Our quest begins with endless whys
Seeking words to make us wise

In Spring

Bright green on each tip makes
spring fir trees look like
ruffled party dresses
They line the road in every size
Here, try one on
Feel the way your fingers
nose, toes and tongue react
Does even your hair tingle?
New growth looks good, feels fine

Like A Memory

Ethereal blue lets you see
Right through to the other side
It is the illusive band seldom seen in a rainbow
An otherworldly hue
It sometimes lights a cloud bank
Once, it was the color of my first memory

I saw my brother's soul at play, clear as firelight
Today, I play with thoughts, as he did blocks...
To find out what we knew

We knew that darkness
drains all color from the world
that dreams are real and we feel
from somewhere high above
We knew that lurking underneath
there's a nameless dread of
what's under the bed
It's at least as bad as
the nightmare fall that wakes us
to creep out seeking solace
in the middle of the night
We knew that love protected us
when we were very small

On A Dark Night

First snow falls
Straight down in weighty packs
White against, and for, the dark gray world
Five weeks till Christmas Eve, my love says
I count... eleven long evenings this month
twenty four even longer ones in December
'Tis the season, the festive, sacred season
For no reason, the first story tugs at me

Not the first Christmas, but the creation ...
How God paused every evening
Looked at each miraculous new thing
Saw that it was good
On the last evening
Indeed... it was very good

This season
I want to pause more often
See what is new... but
Remember the miraculous

Riddled By Stars

Riddled

The egg must have come before the chicken
Because if Humpty Dumpty had a mother
She would have told him,
"Pull yourself together"
He would have
put himself together
and then gone around saying,
"Anything that doesn't kill you outright
is bound to make you all the better for it"

By Stars

In the dead black of a moonless night
The stars reveal a splendor
That makes you think
You're on the brink of being
Far away, tiny, one of billions
Then comes the dawn, and
Life goes on
In closer step with all

Who

Owl's voice calls
Leads me to a forest path
Around and back
Back in time
Driving on a prairie highway
I, mesmerized by
White on white
Earth and sky
Snowdrifts rolling, rolling by...
Snap wide awake when
One of them appears to fly
Wingspan windshield wide
Whirled white cape around a face
Round and staring yellow eyes
Shaman shadow shakes, rattles...
Soars away

Wonders

I don't remember
crawling from the sea
cold blooded
to the warmth of land
I wish I could remember
back to then or even when
at first my blood turned warm
I wonder if I flew?
Were there times I was a cat
or hid while being hunted?
Of course the me who has such thoughts
was never then... except in dreams
But once
What seemed a memory
from millenniums ago
dawned, in my imagination
As a child
I held it soft in snowy mitts
felt a heart's dimensions shift
flower into consciousness

About the Message

Wavelets lap the kayak
Sunshine licks it too

A grebe and I
Observe the sky
Jet trails fan and twist
The breezes play at
Finger painting
White on blue

Double lines converge
Images emerge
Punctuation
Words

It becomes a work of art
The message is this
You've no one to blame
When you're hit by a train

Fear Not

I once thought that knowledge
was the antidote to fear
But that was before the news
filled my head with fearful facts
damned the human race
Information is not knowledge
Wisdom is their very distant relation
Fairy Godmother perhaps?
Fear not, she says, *do not despair*
Wisdom is my given name
My last name is Compassion

Someone Once Said

A poem is like a message in a bottle
Who sends a message in a bottle?
Desperate shipwrecked souls
Children playing on the shore
What do they say?
I am... hear

With All Due Gravity

It seems to me a travesty
to only notice gravity
in the fable of the apple and the sage
for when that apple fell on him...
Slapstick pandemonium!
Apples landing everywhere
The tree shaking with laughter

I only mean to underscore
Newton should get credit for
Both gravity and levity
Now that I think of it
Levity may well be
The great unifying force
Oh I trust that old saw
Love conquers all
But a little levity never hurts

Are We There Yet?

Journey far
Further still
On once again
Until
All of outside
Flooding in
Quiets
to a deep
reflective pool
There
Moonlight bathes each face
There
Every place is home

Yes

Love and fear walk hand in hand
On shifting sands of circumstance
Beside the restless sea
Sometimes Fear grows large and strong
Looks down and sees in his big fist
A tiny trusting hand
He picks up Love
To toss above his head
Her shriek of fright
Turns to delight
As he catches her again
Though stronger now, bigger too
It is as though they've traded places
He is Love, and Fear is caught
In his protective care

Celebrate

Ruby, gold and amber
Rose hips as big as cherries
A last blood red blossom
Fragrance flows
through my veins
to generations
of Grandmothers

I look toward a house
Smoke rises from the chimney
An old wood kitchen stove is
perhaps roasting a turkey
baking pumpkin pies
Soon, family will arrive
for Thanksgiving

Together

Within my many selves there dwell
a muskox and a maiden
a pitcher pouring out its heart
to a talking writing raven
weathered sages
will-o-the wisps
a fire breathing dragon
Horn and spout
scale and doubt
beak and eye together
Journey through the sacred woods
Draw water from its wells
Pilgrims who lodge briefly
within this citadel
Here to live out loud
kindness, stories, laughter
Practice as a daily art
happy ever after

Notes on the Poets:

Mark Mealing is a college professor(retired); folklorist, author, poet, storyteller & Priest (all unretired), & has produced a book & other published poems. He lives quietly in Meadow Creek with two cats, a dog; & a lot of mountains, water & trees.

Anne Heard has worked in early childhood development, recreation therapy, and outdoor education. She loves living in Kaslo with her family and welcomes the opportunity to play and to be with people and the land.

Sheila Murray-Nellis was the first prize winner of the Kootenay Literary Competition in 2010 and again in 2012. She has published two books of poetry: *You Are Meant to Be Like Fire* and *Presence.* She lives in Birchdale, BC.

Robert Banks Foster started publishing poems from coast to coast at the age of 20. He was editor of *Contemporary Verse II* under Dorothy Livesay 1977-85. He is the author of *Across The White Lawn* from Turnstone Press and co translator of Euripides' *The Bacchae* with Margaret Behr to appear shortly.

Sheila Falle: The most interesting thing about me is that I never needed an imaginary friend because I have a twin brother. He is the other half of we in "It Begins" and "Like A Memory." My husband is my love in "On a Dark Night." These poems are ones I know by heart in a way which lets them change as I meditate, subtly reshaping both themselves and my heart. This is how they read today. All were first written down thanks to forming our poetry circle in 2004.

Acknowledgements

With gratitude to the editors of the journals and books where some of these poems previously appeared:

St Katherine's Journal, 2014: "Invisible Highway"

When Words Take Flight: "While Alone, Thoughts Escape"

You Are Meant to Be Like Fire: "Invisible Highway"; "While Alone, Thoughts Escape"; "To You Who Lives There Now"

Presence: "An Ebb and Flow and Then We Break Through"

"Through Darkness the Hidden Beauty Rises" was commissioned and read at the June 4 and 5, 2016, performances of Kaslo Community Choir in Argenta and Kaslo, BC, directed by Karen Behn and Tamara SunSong

The Prairie Journal, #57, 2012: "Crocus"

Elephant Mountain, No. 1 2013/2014: "Water Sequence"

Anglican Theological Review, Vol. LX, No. 1, January 1978: "Eschatology"

The Fiddlehead, No. 147, Spring 1986: "Finally"

Grain, Vol. 21, #3, Fall 1993: "For George"

The Malahat Review, #67, 1984: "Trapped in the Story"

www.ingramcontent.com/pod-product-compliance
Lightning Source LLC
Chambersburg PA
CBHW020920090426
42736CB00008B/724